General editor: Graham Handley MA Ph.D.

Brodie's Notes on J. M. Synge's
The Playboy of the Western World

W. S. Bunnell MA FCP

MACMILLAN

© W. S. Bunnell 1978

All rights reserved. No reproduction, copy or transmission of
this publication may be made without written permission.

No paragraph of this publication may be reproduced, copied or
transmitted save with written permission or in accordance with
the provisions of the Copyright, Designs and Patents Act 1988,
or under the terms of any licence permitting limited copying
issued by the Copyright Licensing Agency, 90 Tottenham Court
Road, London W1P 9HE.

Any person who does any unauthorised act in relation to this
publication may be liable to criminal prosecution and civil
claims for damages.

First published 1978 by Pan Books Ltd

This revised edition published 1993 by
THE MACMILLAN PRESS LTD
Houndmills, Basingstoke, Hampshire RG21 2XS
and London
Companies and representatives
throughout the world

ISBN 0-333-58206-3

Typeset by Footnote Graphics, Warminster, Wiltshire
Printed in Great Britain by
Cox & Wyman Ltd, Reading

Contents

Preface by the general editor 5

The author and his work 7

The *Playboy* riots 16

Plot and theme 19
Plot 19
Theme 20

Act summaries, critical commentary, textual notes and revision questions 23

The characters 40
Christy Mahon 40
Old Mahon 43
Pegeen Mike (Margaret Flaherty) 45
Widow Quin 47
Shawn Keogh 49
Michael James Flaherty 50

Style 51
The writing of the play 51
Peasant speech 52
Vocabulary and use of words 53
Use of dialect 55

General questions and sample answer in note form 57

Further reading 59

Preface

The intention throughout this study aid is to stimulate and guide, to encourage your involvement in the book, and to develop informed responses and a sure understanding of the main details.

Brodie's Notes provide a clear outline of the play or novel's plot, followed by act, scene, or chapter summaries and/or commentaries. These are designed to emphasize the most important literary and factual details. Poems, stories or non-fiction texts combine brief summary with critical commentary on individual aspects or common features of the genre being examined. Textual notes define what is difficult or obscure and emphasize literary qualities. Revision questions are set at appropriate points to test your ability to appreciate the prescribed book and to write accurately and relevantly about it.

In addition, each of these Notes includes a critical appreciation of the author's art. This covers such major elements as characterization, style, structure, setting and themes. Poems are examined technically – rhyme, rhythm, for instance. In fact, any important aspect of the prescribed work will be evaluated. The aim is to send you back to the text you are studying.

Each study aid concludes with a series of general questions which require a detailed knowledge of the book: some of these questions may invite comparison with other books, some will be suitable for coursework exercises, and some could be adapted to work you are doing on another book or books. Each study aid has been adapted to meet the needs of the current examination requirements. They provide a basic, individual and imaginative response to the work being studied, and it is hoped that they will stimulate you to acquire disciplined reading habits and critical fluency.

Graham Handley 1990

As references are made to particular Acts, the Notes may be used with any edition of the play.

The author and his work

John Millington Synge was born at Rathfarnham, near Dublin, on 16 April 1871. His family were strongly Protestant, and included no fewer than five bishops in their past. The family had been landowners with large estates in Ireland though these were small by the time Synge was born.

Synge's family was English by descent and Protestant in religion. The Anglo-Irish had been associated with the ruling classes of Ireland since the English conquest in the time of the first Elizabeth. They did not consciously identify themselves with England or the English, but were nevertheless a distinctive group, set apart from the rural and Roman Catholic majority. Class was strengthened by religion; social divisions were more rigid than in nineteenth-century England. It was into this background that Synge was born, as indeed also was George Bernard Shaw.

His father, a barrister, died when Synge was one year old: he was brought up by his mother, a convinced and extreme evangelical Protestant who unceasingly preached the dangers of Hell to her children.

John's health was poor; he suffered from asthma. He was largely educated at home, and led a solitary life in which an interest in natural history and walking played a large part. Perhaps, like Christy Mahon, 'he'd be fooling over little birds he had – finches and felts.'

When he was fourteen he read a book by the naturalist Charles Darwin, whose ideas on the origin of man disturbed the accepted views of the time and led many to question the truth of the Bible teaching and their own beliefs. It had a similar effect on Synge; before he was seventeen he had, after much tortured thinking, renounced the Christian faith.

Synge regarded this loss of belief as of enormous importance in separating him from his background. 'By it I had laid a chasm between my present and my past, and between myself and my kindred and friends. Till I was twenty-three I never met, or at least knew, a man or woman who shared my opinions.'

Nature became an important influence in his life. Like the poet Wordsworth, he sought his faith and the meaning of life in the beauty and the romance of nature. Music was also a consolation to him.

In 1888 he went to Trinity College, Dublin. 'All my time was given to the violin and vague private reading, and the work for my examinations received just enough attention to attain the pass standard' is how Synge described his time at University. It was at this time he developed a consciousness of nationalism. 'Everything Irish became sacred,' he wrote. In 1889 he attended lectures at the Royal Academy of Music, and considered making music his profession. This further alarmed his mother. Synge could play the violin, the flute, the penny whistle and the piano. At Trinity he studied Irish and Hebrew, though he learned more about Ireland from the books he read than from his teachers. He spent his holidays with his family in the Irish countryside, and he developed an interest in the Wicklow peasants.

His first love was Cherry Matheson, to whom he proposed marriage in 1896. The frustrations of his love for her are mirrored in his first play, *When the Moon Has Set*. Her father was a fervent member of the Plymouth Brethren; and she refused Synge because of his atheism. Her rejection intensified the conflict between his intellectual opinions and his personal feelings.

In 1893, Synge went to Germany to study music, and stayed at Oberworth and Würzburg. This was the final breach with his family. He soon decided to abandon music as a profession, and in 1894 he went to Paris. Here he took lodgings, attended the Sorbonne, began to write, and taught some English. He was very poor; sometimes he had to stay in bed to keep warm during the cold winter days. His annuity of about £40 was inadequate for his needs. One observer wrote about the relationship of Synge and Stephen MacKenna, later an Irish Nationalist and writer, 'How do those two young men live? Oh, Synge lives on what MacKenna lends him, and MacKenna lives on what Synge pays him back.' At this time, Synge read widely in European literature.

Synge had developed into a silent, reserved and isolated young man – qualities he was to show throughout his life. He gave the appearance of an observer of life rather than a participator in it. 'He had under charming and modest manners, in almost all things of life, a complete absorption in his own dream,' W. B. Yeats noted. Yet Synge was kind and considerate. John Masefield, the English poet, said he never saw Synge angry. He could speak and communicate with close friends. Masefield testified:

> And now I miss that friend who used to walk
> Home to my lodgings with me, deep in talk.

In physique he was big and strong; his head was large; his eyes were luminous; his complexion was pale. His hair was dark and his moustache thick and heavy. James Joyce in *Ulysses* ascribed to him a 'harsh gargoyle face'. Bernard Shaw said he had a face like a blacking-brush.

Similar in fame to Stanley's meeting with Livingstone is that of Synge with W. B. Yeats in Paris. Yeats met Synge for the first time in December 1896. Synge had just arrived from Italy and was now 'reading French literature and writing morbid and melancholy verse'. When Yeats learned that Synge had studied Irish at Trinity College, he 'urged him to go to the Aran Islands and find a life that had never been expressed in literature, instead of a life where all had been expressed.' Yeats continued: 'I did not divine his genius, but I felt he needed something to take him out of his morbidity and melancholy. Perhaps I would have given the same advice to any young Irish writer who knew Irish, for I had been that summer upon Inishmaan and Inishmore, and was full of the subject.' It was a year, however, before Synge took this advice, and stayed for a time in an Aran cottage. An Irish actor friend asserted that Synge found life there interesting but not very enjoyable, and that it was probably made tolerable only because he was able to spend part of each year in Paris.

Yeats also involved Synge in the Irish League, founded by Yeats and the beautiful Maud Gonne, to further the cause of Irish nationalism and independence. Synge attended the weekly meetings in Paris, but soon resigned: he had little interest in politics – Yeats later said that Synge was incapable of thinking a political thought. John Masefield asserted that he was the only Irishman he had ever met who cared nothing for politics and religion. Lady Gregory thought he looked on politics 'with a sort of tolerant indifference'.

Similarly, Synge was indifferent to the religious strife in the Ireland of his time. His own loss of belief had divorced him from the Protestantism of his youth, and he was indifferent to Roman Catholicism. He seemed little interested in the compelling impact that religion had upon the life, thought and attitudes of the peasants. He is content to record, as in *The Playboy of the Western World*, the people's references to God, the Roman Catholic Church, the Virgin Mary and the Saints – though his recording is so plain and matter-of-fact that it seems shot through with an irony that was taken as an attack upon religion.

In 1897, he was operated on for a lump that had formed in the side of his neck. This was the beginning of a long record of serious illness that was to dog him throughout the rest of his short life.

Synge made, in all, five visits to Aran. In this isolated island situated in the Atlantic, he made his first prolonged and serious study of Irish-peasant life. The germ of many ideas that were later to find expression in *The Playboy* came to him in Aran – the instinctive desire to protect the criminal; the rich development of the individual; the harshness of the life; the development of the imagination; the love of stories; a ready acceptance of the supernatural; and a savage brutality. Out of his experiences in Aran and in Wicklow came two early works, *The Aran Islands* and *In Wicklow and West Kerry*.

In 1898, he first visited Lady Gregory at Coole Park, the beginning of his connection with the Irish theatre movement. *When the Moon Has Set* was Synge's first play. Both plot and ideas were strongly autobiographical. The play was written between 1896 and 1903, and there are several versions of it. In 1901 *The Aran Islands* was rejected by Grant Richards for publication and *When the Moon has Set* by Lady Gregory for the Irish Literary Theatre. In 1902 *The Aran Islands* was also rejected by Fisher Unwin. It was in this year that Synge turned to the Irish scene for his dramatic inspiration: *Riders to the Sea* and *In The Shadow of the Glen* were completed; and he also began *The Tinker's Wedding*.

With *Riders to the Sea* (first performed in 1904), Synge achieved immediate greatness. This is no apprentice work but a consummate masterpiece. It is the one play set on Aran; and it expresses the intense sense of realism, the constant presence of death and the overwhelming and malignant influence of fate over man's life that has encouraged some critics to describe the play as a Greek tragedy in a peasant setting.

In *In The Shadow of the Glen* (first performed in 1903) Synge turned from the sombre death-ridden world of *Riders to the Sea* to the distinctive form of comedy that was to be most representative of his writing. The plot was a classic one of farce – the husband pretending to be dead in order to discover his wife with her lover. The theme of adultery was attacked in the press and in the first performance a pattern was established that was ultimately to find its most forceful expression in the reaction to *The Playboy of the Western World*.

The Tinker's Wedding was not finished until 1906. It has been little regarded by the critics; and it was not produced by the Abbey Theatre until sixty-four years after its publication in 1907. *The Well of the Saints* was performed in 1905, with only a handful of people present. It has not been a popular play, and has been seldom produced – its depressing atmosphere and unpleasant characters are in direct contrast to the vital imagination shown in *The Playboy of the Western World*.

During these years the Irish Literary Theatre was looking for, and finally found, a permanent home. Annie Horniman, founder of the Manchester Repertory Theatre, generously assisted in its provision. The Abbey Theatre seated five hundred: productions were initially amateur; but later, with the support of Yeats, Lady Gregory and Synge as directors, the Abbey Theatre Company was formed. It was always a centre of controversy. Ironically, it was the visits to England that provided the money to maintain the company and its theatre. It was the emphasis on realism in setting, language and scenery that made a startling impact on English audiences. Under William Fay, its first manager, a natural approach to acting was developed. The realism of the plays presented was often in conflict with the lofty ideals of the nationalists as well as the traditional supporters of religion. Even Maud Gonne later protested against the attack on womanhood in *In The Shadow of the Glen*.

Synge and Sean O'Casey made a permanent contribution to the English-speaking theatre. Synge towered above the other dramatists with whom he was associated. Yeats was disillusioned by the realism of the Abbey Theatre and retreated into the verse play which was designed for reading rather than acting. Synge had a mastery of technique and a sense of theatre that was lacking in Yeats. Synge was saved from the provincialism that beset some of the Abbey dramatists by his intimate knowledge of continental literature; he was always able to infuse a universal quality into the provincial world of the peasant. Yet he had an eye for detail and a gift of close observation that enabled him to combine realism with poetry and imagination in a way that Yeats never did. The period of collaboration with Synge became, for Yeats, a significant part of his life.

> And that enquiring man John Synge comes next
> That dying chose the living world for text.

A nineteen-year-old actress at the Abbey Theatre, Molly Allgood, whom Synge met through her walk-on part in *The Well of the Saints*, attracted Synge and he soon fell in love with her. Synge was tortured by the ideas of the difference in their ages, as he was by his ill health, which he considered to be an obstacle to their relationship. Molly was also a Roman Catholic, and separated from Synge by birth, background and education. It was to prove a tempestuous relationship. Even when Synge was almost thirty, he feared the reaction of his family to a Roman Catholic and an actress; and the difference in their ages made him jealous. (Yeats and Lady Gregory were both worried about the relationship, partly because Synge was a director of the theatre and Molly one of its employees.) The pair found happiness in walking together in Wicklow; but they often quarrelled over Synge's jealousy and Molly's lack of consideration and concern. Molly had a quick temper; she was volatile, independent, restless and ambitious. They became secretly engaged in 1906.

It was during his relationship with Molly that Synge wrote *The Playboy of the Western World* (he had made his preliminary notes for the play in 1904). At this time he was suffering from the pain caused by a growth in his side. His mother had moved to Glendalough House in Glenageary, where Synge had a room and where he worked on *The Playboy*. He wrote constantly to Molly, passionate letters looking forward desperately to their next meeting. He implored her to educate herself by reading. At this time he told his family about Molly; they were less hostile than he expected. But the relationship with Molly continued to be marked by quarrels, jealousy and misunderstanding. She resented his attempts to educate her and was angry at his lack of enthusiasm for her achievements on the stage. However, at times, when he grew depressed at his slowness in completing *The Playboy*, she supported and encouraged him. Then Synge had a second operation for the growth in his neck. There were troubles at the Abbey Theatre, in which Yeats, Lady Gregory, Miss Horniman and Synge were all involved in differences of opinion about its present and future policy. Then rehearsals of *The Playboy of the Western World* were begun, and the play was first performed on 26 January 1907, with Molly Allgood as Pegeen Mike. The *Playboy* riots are now part of theatrical history. It was not until it was performed in June at Oxford and London that the greatness of the play was recognized. It was also in 1907 that *The Aran Islands* was at last published.

After leaving hospital Synge decided that he and Molly should be married. The writing of *Deirdre of the Sorrows* was now under way. Neither in the treatment of the theme nor in the use of language was the play completely successful. The inspiration was to some extent autobiographical; his love for Molly and his consciousness of the nearness of his own death were the emotional background to the writing of *Deirdre*.

Exploratory surgery showed that an operation would not cure the growth in his side. In 1908 he paid a visit to Germany, and while he was there his mother died. His poems were accepted for publication in this year. In January 1909, he entered the Elpis Nursing Home. His strength was not sufficient for him to complete *Deirdre*. He spoke of it as his last disappointment: he knew he was dying. Just before he died, he asked the nurse to move his bed into a room where he could see the Wicklow mountains. The mountains could not be seen from the windows, and Synge could not stand up to see them: his last wish was frustrated. He had been visited by Molly every day in the period before he died; his relations, though they called at the hospital to enquire after his health, had not seen him. He died in the early morning of 24 March 1909.

Deirdre of the Sorrows was edited by Lady Gregory, Yeats and Molly. It was performed in January 1910. Deirdre was played by Molly, who also directed the production.

Synge's dramatic production was small; its distinctive Irish and peasant quality has narrowed the width of its appeal. Yet it is the mastery Synge reveals within these limitations that constitutes the greatness of his work. *The Playboy of the Western World* is universal in its appeal.

The *Playboy* riots

When *The Playboy of the Western World* went into rehearsal, there were hesitations about its possible impact. Lady Gregory and W. B. Yeats considered that it contained far too much bad language and too many violent oaths. Lady Gregory on the night before the production wanted many more cuts, and removed many phrases herself. At rehearsal Fay, who produced the play, was unhappy about its future. Synge was still smarting under the hostility with which *The Well of the Saints* had been received. 'The next play I write I will make sure will annoy them,' he said to Fay. As soon as Fay saw the script he knew the reaction against it would be violent unless it was altered drastically: 'Many and many a time,' he wrote, 'I strove with him, using all the arguments I could muster, to get him to see that if you attack your audience you must expect them to retaliate.' In particular Fay begged him to make Pegeen a 'decent likeable country girl' and remove the scene in the last act where Christy is burned with the turf. Synge was not to be moved. That was his play, he said.

The play was given its first performance on Saturday, 26 January 1907, at the Abbey Theatre, Dublin. The first act was well received. The second act began with the audience laughing but, with the entry of Widow Quin, there was a growing restlessness. Much of this opposition was to the swearing, and in particular to the use of the word 'bloody'. It must be remembered that when Shaw, in *Pygmalion* many years later, makes his heroine Miss Eliza Doolittle say once, 'Not bloody likely', he does so conscious that the impact will be dramatic and startling. Yet at the end of the second act Lady Gregory sent a telegram to Yeats to assure him that the play was a great success.

The line spoken by Christy, 'It's Pegeen I'm seeking only,

and what'd I care if you brought me a drift of chosen females standing in their shifts itself?', that moved the audience to a frenzy of rage. Lady Gregory sent another telegram to Yeats, 'Audience broke up in disorder at the word shift.' There were fights in the stalls. The actors could not be heard.

On Sunday, the *Freeman's Journal* complained:

Everything is a b— this or a b— that and into this picturesque dialogue names that should be used with respect and reverence are frequently introduced. Enough! ... The piece is announced to run for a week: it is too be hoped it will be instantly withdrawn.

One critic at least stated that the play included an objectionable word that was not there, and he had to withdraw the charge. But this was typical of the attacks, which were based on the assumption that nothing was too bad or too outrageous to appear in the play.

On the following Monday the play was again presented. The riot began when Christy tells how he killed his father. Fay appealed to the audience, saying that some members of the audience had paid to see the play and that those who did not wish to stay were free to leave. No one left. The play continued, but little of what the actors were saying could be heard. There were cries of 'Kill the author.' The police were sent for, but this display of force failed to bring calm. In an interview with the Dublin *Evening Telegraph* Synge stated that the police were instructed to interfere only if there was personal violence: it was at his and Lady Gregory's request that they withdrew.

The fighting had spread to the streets outside. An eyewitness described Synge as watching and listening to all this without showing any trace of emotion. Yeats, however, considered that Synge was 'much shaken' by the *Playboy* riots. On Tuesday the riots were worse. Some students from Trinity to whom Yeats gave free tickets sang, for some strange reason, 'God Save the King'. Yeats again called the police, who this time made arrests. Speaking from the stage, Yeats asserted that, 'The country that condescends either to bully or to permit itself to be bullied soon ceases to have any fine qualities.' He asserted their determination to continue. Synge also stated, 'We shall go on with the play to the very end in spite of all. I don't care a rap.'

On Wednesday and Thursday, with an increase in the number of police, the audience was quieter. In the police court on Wednesday morning there was some evidence of a conspiracy against the play and there were some leading nationalists among the accused. On Friday and Saturday the play could be heard. The controversy had shifted to the columns of the press. In *Sinn Fein* the play was described as 'a vile and inhuman story told in the foulest language'.

Thus, a play about the conditions of the Irish peasantry in Ireland's own theatre was violently attacked by nationalists and defended by the power of the English government! *The Playboy*, in its attempt to portray the real life, emotions and attitudes of the peasants had offended the idealized sensibilities of those who could not or would not face the realities of Irish peasant life. They resented the play's references to the Catholic Church and to God. The attitude to marriage in the play was far removed from the Church's sacramental view. The play's presentation of patricide as the stuff of comedy was found objectionable. The view the play presented of Ireland was attacked as being unpatriotic.

Plot and theme

Plot

The plot of *The Playboy of the Western World* is tightly controlled and observes the unities of time, place and action of Greek tragedy. The action is centred almost wholly around Christy. All the other characters revolve around him and have their identity through him. The whole action takes place in the one room of the shebeen, even though the impression of constant movement is given through the intensity of the imaginative description. Such is the account of the sports, the second attack on Old Mahon, and even the drunkenness of the men at Kate Cassidy's wake. The unity of place is an opportunity for Synge to exploit the imaginative power of the language. At first Synge had considered having Old Mahon return at the door of the church as Christy is about to marry Pegeen; he had planned the opening of the play in the field where Christy had quarrelled with his father.

The time taken by the action is less than twenty-four hours. Christy arrives during the evening and he and his father leave in the early evening of the following day. Much has happened, much has changed, but it is all within a very short time. This gives to the play the feeling of pace and excitement.

The mechanics of the plot concern Christy's supposed killing of his father and the events that follow from that. The plot is substantially the ironic examination of a story, the story of a patricide that Synge had heard in the Aran Islands. The story is examined from several points of view. It is first of all presented directly. The irony of the play is not in the ready acceptance of the murder and the subsequent admiration that Christy receives as a result. The real irony is in the inability to accept the brutal reality of the murder when Christy re-enacts it in a desperate attempt to regain Pegeen's love and the men's admiration by making the story an actuality. That is why, except to the realist Widow Quin, Christy's achievements in the sports count for less than the story of his father's killing. The story is welcomed: the result is rejected.

Theme

The extracting of a 'theme' from this play is a difficult pursuit. It is more a matter of different kinds of *meaning* and *approach*. On one level the story is about a peasant community: the poverty and the harshness of life; the arranged marriage; the drinking, boasting, savagery – they are all there. Those who were hostile to the play were well aware of how powerful and unflattering is Synge's picture of an Irish peasant community. However, from this narrow picture emerges a drama and a group of characters which have a universal appeal.

Synge himself wrote that the play was 'not a play with "a purpose" in the modern sense of the word, but although parts of it are, or are meant to be, extravagant comedy, still a great deal more that is behind it is perfectly serious when looked at in a certain light. That is often the case, I think, with comedy.' Synge did not deny that one theme in the play may have been a warning about the future of an Ireland that was witnessing the emigration of its best and most vigorous people and weakening itself by the custom of arranged and loveless marriages. Certainly the triangular relationship between Pegeen and Shawn and Christy would fit the latter. But this is straining the play's dramatic purpose. There is little indication in Synge's writings of the meanings of his plays. 'I follow Goethe's rule,' he said on one occasion, 'to tell no one what one means in one's writing.'

There is no doubt that in this play, as indeed in many plays and novels, there is a great deal of Synge's own feelings and attitudes. The constant fear of being alone expressed in the play is one example. The ironic approach to life is yet another. The poetry and the quarrels that mark the love of

Christy and Pegeen may be autobiographical. 'The Playboy's real name was Synge,' said Bernard Shaw, 'and the famous libel on Ireland (and who is Ireland that she should not be libelled as other countries by her great comedians?) was the truth about the world.' Much of the savagery may spring from Synge's own fascination with the violence of life, a preoccupation not unusual in men who suffer from serious illness.

Fundamentally, the play is a comedy in its feeling and approach. But it is not pure comedy, inhabiting a world of unalloyed joy and delight – few comedies do. Synge, like Shakespeare, mixes laughter with the shadows and the harsher realities of life. The real test of comedy is the laughter it provokes, and anyone who has seen a performance of the play or the film cannot be left in any doubt about the laughter provoked by *The Playboy*.

The comedy is of all kinds – character, situation and dialogue. Often more than one is combined. Sara's comment, 'Them that kills their fathers is a vain lot surely', is a verbal extra to the comedy inherent in the situation of Christy's being discovered looking at himself in the mirror. Christy's indignant declaration that he would never use weapons as he had no licence and he was a 'law-fearing man' is ironic humour at its keenest – coming as it does in the context of his description of murdering his father.

There is much comedy of situation. Such are Pegeen's breaking in upon Christy, the Widow Quin and the girls; the inconvenient appearances of Old Mahon; and the use of drunkenness. Some of the situations indeed come very close to the too obviously contrived. They are, however, effective on the stage and add to the excitement of the plot.

Satire there is in abundance, based on Synge's unerringly accurate observation of the Irish peasant. It offended the early audiences; later audiences have found it very acceptable comedy. Christy's declaration that he killed his father with the help of God is one example of Synge's ironic observation of the peasant speech (shot through with constant reference to God, the Virgin Mary and the Saints and a satire on their largely mechanical and unthinking use).

It is the last act that is most difficult to include easily in any comic definition. The torturing of Christy and his rejection by Pegeen certainly lie outside the bounds and the feeling of comedy. Their justification lies in the development and realization of character. There is no doubt that the salvation of Christy and the events consequent upon it are more important than keeping the play within the bounds of any academic definition of comedy.

Pegeen's wild lament again does not fit into the world of comedy. In the true spirit of comedy Christy would have returned and married her. Pegeen's realization is fractionally too late. She has served her purpose in terms of Christy's development. He will 'go romancing through a romping lifetime from this hour to the drawing of the judgement day' without Pegeen. His resolution and her loss have the finality of tragedy about them, rather than the temporary and forward-looking tying up of the comic ending.

Act summaries, critical commentary, textual notes and revision questions

Act 1

The play opens in the bar of an inn. Pegeen Mike, a girl of twenty, is speaking to Shawn Keogh, a stout young man, who hopes to marry her. She objects to her father's leaving her alone and in charge of the inn on a long dark night. They are waiting for a dispensation from the Church to marry in Lent. Shawn is unwilling to stay the night, for fear of what the priest will say. He mentions that on his way here he has heard a man groaning in the ditch. Pegeen's father, Michael James, enters with two friends. When Pegeen complains about being left alone, they try to prevent Shawn from leaving, but he escapes.

Christy Mahon enters – the man Shawn had heard in the ditch. He confesses that he has killed his father in a fit of anger. Their estimate of Christy is immensely raised when they hear this. They offer Christy hospitality and work. He says he has been walking for eleven days since he killed his father. The men then leave, secure in the knowledge that Pegeen will be safe. Shawn now offers to stay, but is summarily ejected by the scornful Pegeen. The relationship between Christy and Pegeen immediately reveals appreciation and sympathy between them. Their conversation is interrupted by the Widow Quin, who has been sent by Shawn and the priest to take Christy to lodge with her. After a lively exchange of words and insults between the two women, the Widow Quin, after offering to stay, finally leaves. Christy goes to bed, feeling that fortune is smiling on him, glorying in two women fighting over him, and wishing he had 'killed' his father before.

Notice the authenticity of the scene, which is enhanced by the opening relaxed dialogue, a contrast with so much of what is to come. The prose is rhythmic but with something of poetry in it, and Pegeen is in control of the situation from the beginning. She is playing on the sympathy of Shawn, but gets instead his wish to marry her: the dialogue about the Pope and the Church is ironic, but notice again Pegeen's description of the people, a natural transition to peasant realism. As she continues to moan about being alone we wonder if her apprehension is genuine or simulated. Her use of the word 'murderer' rouses tension, and this is fuelled by Shawn's account of what he has heard, which prepares us for the main action. Shawn's timidity – and Pegeen's courage – are admirably brought out. But with the reappearance of her father she is able to act up completely, conjuring the possibility of violence and rape, and thus provoking a further display of Shawn's timidity, here in the name of religion. Michael reveals almost in passing that he has heard the incident in the ditch, thus again arousing audience expectation. Obviously religious morality is being satirised at the same time, through Shawn's constant reference, and Irish life is being captured – or caricatured – in the process. There is some farce too in Shawn leaving but leaving his coat.

Shawn's return raises the dramatic temperature. We feel we are on the edge of action (as does Shawn), and Synge's dramatic craftsmanship is in evidence. Christy's change from small voice to mention of the police adds to the tension, and the black comedy begins as they question Christy with a view to finding out what he has done. Christy is adept at baiting them, his wonderful remark about being a decent lad showing his own appreciation of his position. He runs the social gamut of possibilities – he is winding up his audience and enjoying it. There is the fine irony too of his telling Pegeen that she is not speaking the truth, while his account of the murder – the supposed murder – takes its humour from the cutting edge of the supposed motivation. The positive comedy is that there is no sense of shock in his audience (though a theatre audience might of course be reacting differently): they merely proceed to the next round of sensation, which is to discover how he (supposedly) did it. Again we are aware of the delight in vicarious experience on their behalf.

Once this is revealed Michael's action in having Christy's glass filled is evidence of respect. Snide remarks about police caution follow, Pegeen recurs naturally to her own coming loneliness, reversing conventional appraisals of having a murderer in the house by saying that she would feel protected if she had one. This is audacious humour, undermining the fabric of respectability, as Shawn timidly points out. The dialogue between Pegeen and Christy shows at this stage that they are two of a kind, with Pegeen intent on finding out as much as she can about Christy, and the latter waxing ironic and constantly reiterating the main outline of his story. Conventional romance is also being turned on its head. Each needs the other, and each is directly provocative. Pegeen is disappointed that there has been apparently no romance in Christy's life.

Christy's regaling of her with stories of his poaching exploits smack not so much of exaggeration as deprivation, but the account of the violence and the drinking (and the loneliness and monotony of such a life) comes through vividly. One can see why this particular aspect of Irish life gave so much offence: in a sense, Synge was holding up the mirror to his audience and showing them what they didn't want to see. It also accounts for the play's universality – it is a direct appraisal of human nature shorn of romance. The movement to farce comes suddenly with Christy clinging to Pegeen after expressing so much bravery, reduced to fear by the knocking at the door.

Widow Quin's entrance is comic anti-climax. But soon the power of the priesthood and the need for respectability (outward but not inward) is seen again. Notice how possessive each woman is about Christy, without really knowing him but only knowing what he is supposed to have done. The insults between the two women are really a trial of strength to see who will succeed in taking over Christy. Pegeen's triumph is evidence of her power and sexuality. Christy is temporarily troubled by the reference to Pegeen's coming marriage, and the act ends on a note of sick humour with Christy's meditation. The impact of the play would be immediate. The combination of poetry and rawness in the dialogue makes an immediate dramatic focus, and the characters interact directly. Note the tense economy of the style.

Shebeen A common public house; here a room with a somewhat primitive bar set up in it.
turf Used as a substitute for coal.
porter A bitter dark-brown beer.
creel cart A farm cart with high movable sides used for animals etc.
wake A farewell party for the dead.
scruff Lower part.
dispensation Permission (in this case to marry in Lent) from the Roman Catholic Church.
peeler Policeman (after Sir Robert Peel who established the force).
maiming ewes A common method of revenge in a rural community.
whisht Be quiet.
Stooks of the Dead Woman Rocks on the shore, which look like sheaves of cut corn leaning against each other to dry, in this case looking like dead women. They are here the name of existing rocks.
tinkers Menders of pots, pans etc. They travelled about and were regarded as thieves.
militia Part-time soldiers.
gripe Bottom.
St Joseph A mocking of the Irish peasant's practice of invoking the help of the Saints. Here Shawn invokes four for good measure.
penny pot-boy Server in a public house.
bellman cf. bell-buoy which gives a warning and is rung by the waves.
polis Police.
bona fide A traveller to whom it was legal to serve drinks outside licensing hours.

broken harvest Bad harvests caused much suffering in Ireland.
ended wars These cast soldiers onto the labour market.
strong farmer Farmer with a good farm and land.
butt of his tail-pocket The bottom of the pocket of a swallow-tailed coat, then much worn for formal occasions.
bailiffs Officers who took possession of land or houses in case of debt.
agents Paid agents, similar to bailiffs but employed by landowners.
Luthers Protestants, after Martin Luther, the founder of German protestantism.
Boers Settlers in South Africa of Dutch descent. The Boer War was fought in 1881 and from 1899–1902. This is introduced into the play by Synge as a reference to Arthur Lynch whom Synge knew in Paris and who fought for the Boers during the South African War.
Kruger Paul Krüger (1825–1904) was President of the Transvaal republic and one of the main leaders of the Boers.
I killed my poor father In *The Aran Islands* Synge tells the story of a Connaught man who killed his father with the blow of a spade. The islanders hid him until he was shipped to America. 'This impulse to protect the criminal,' he writes, 'is universal in the west. It seems partly due to the association between justice and the hated English jurisdiction, but more directly to the primitive feeling of these people. If a man has killed his father, and is already sick and broken with remorse, they can see no reason why he should be dragged away and killed by the law.'
law-fearing man Irony which emphasizes the attitude to the murder.
from the licence To save paying the licence.
loy Spade with a long thin blade for digging peat. The extent of this blow amusingly increased later with each re-telling of the story.
sense of Solomon King of Israel, renowned for his wisdom.
poteen Whiskey illegally distilled, usually from potatoes.
pitchpike Fork used for hay.
loosed khaki cut-throats Soldiers from the Boer War.
drouthy Thirsty.
quality name Aristocratic.
the world 'The world' is loosely used to refer to any part outside the particular parish. On Aran Synge noted this use of the word.

It has a fascination, remoteness and a vague geographical meaning for these untravelled peasant folk. Christy's journey is regarded as a long one.

scribs of bog Strips of wet peat-land.
streeleen Gossip.
Owen Roe O'Sullivan or the poets of the Dingle Bay O'Sullivan was an Irish Robert Burns. He was the best known of all the Munster poets. He was poor, witty and wicked; he loved the girls and hated foreigners. He died young in about 1784. Dingle Bay is situated in Kerry.
St Martin's Day 11 November, traditionally reputed to be a period of late fine spells.
gaudy officer A reference to the brilliant colours in the dress of officers at the time.
banbhs Piglets.
I've their word I've their command.
priesteen Little priest, used contemptuously by Widow Quin.
penny poet Ballad writer.
overed Recovered from it.
man Husband.
Christian Human being.
grass tobacco Dried tobacco leaf not properly cured.
liefer Rather.
Sheepskin parchment The dispensation to marry referred to at the beginning of Act 1. See note p. 26.

Revision questions on Act 1

1 Describe the difference between Pegeen's attitude to Shawn and to Christy.
2 Give an account of the changes of attitude towards Christy between his first entrance and the men leaving.
3 What incidents do you find especially amusing in the first act? Show how they add to the comedy.
4 Describe the character of Christy as shown in the first act.

Act 2

Christy meditates on his good fortune while he performs small tasks in the shebeen. He admires himself in the looking-glass, but is interrupted in this by the entry of Susan Brady, Honor Blake and Sara Tansey, who have come to look upon, and bring gifts to, the man who has murdered his father. Christy enlarges on the story of how he killed his father. They and the Widow Quin who has joined them listen eagerly. Susan sees in him a possible second husband for the Widow Quin. They all then link arms and drink together.

At this moment Pegeen enters. She is very angry, and drives them all out. Then she turns on Christy with all the full force of her anger: she lashes him with her scorn and terrifies him by her graphic description of hanging. Full of self-pity for his loneliness, Christy offers to go: Pegeen relents.

Shawn enters to tell Pegeen that her sheep are in Jimmy's field. While she is out, Shawn offers Christy half of a ticket to the United States; new clothes; his blessing and perhaps that of Father Reilly – if Christy will disappear and leave Shawn free to marry Pegeen. Widow Quin encourages Christy to try on the clothes. (Shawn enlists the aid of Widow Quin by offering her substantial rewards for her help, perhaps the chance to marry Christy herself.) Her attempt is interrupted by the appearance of Old Mahon looking for his son. His head is bandaged but he is very much alive. He contrasts the Christy he knows as a son with the one we know he has changed into, the Playboy of the Western World. Christy realizes that, if Pegeen sees his father, all will be finished between them. Widow Quin offers herself and her house to him; but it is Pegeen he wants. She good-naturedly agrees to aid him by saying nothing to Pegeen and swearing that Old Mahon is a maniac and is not his father. The girls return to bring Christy to the sports.

Since the scene is the same, we are able to contemplate Christy as he contemplates the tremendous (by his standards) potential of the place. His inherent idleness, the changed conditions of his life in this possible future, also have something of pathos about them. With the entrance of the girls he makes a comic exit – an effective contrast with the image of himself as the killer of his father which has drawn on him so much attention. The girls represent credulous gossipy reactions in a small community. They also make the most of the situation, their presents being an invitation to confidences (and possibly even to courtship – men are hard to come by). All the while the ironic humour of the idea – welcoming a (supposed) murderer – is playing over the scene. Christy indulges his story, obviously embroidering it as he goes, and he has two audiences, one on stage and one in the auditorium. He doesn't hesitate to make the worst of his father, but his narrative is vivid, murderous and impressive, creating an admiring response where, in a conventional play, the response would be condemnatory. Sara's toast indicates the extremes to which Synge is going in a kind of black comedy which is baiting his audience. Pegeen's entrance effectively stops the farce, but her reminder of the sports gives promise of further dramatic action. Pegeen now takes over, and Christy has to try to rise to the challenge by picking up the loy: but she is mistress of the situation despite all Christy's distortions. The account of the hanging reduces him completely.

She emphasizes the risks he is taking by talking (Synge is mocking the Irish capacity for fluency and exaggeration) but she is overcome by Christy's poetic – unconsciously poetic – description of the loneliness of his life. The deadly, killing monotony is apparent, but he too is adept at change, and flatters her with another onset of fluency. Appeased, mollified, Pegeen reveals that she too has been telling stories. Christy's response is grateful, lyrical, sexual, a little too much for Pegeen to take, although she is aware that he may be tempted away from her by the widow or the girls.

With the arrival of Shawn and the Widow Quin the pace of the play quickens, and we are aware of mixed motives at work, with Shawn bribing the widow as well as trying to bribe Christy. There is a terrible irony in Shawn making the gesture of hanging in view of Christy's fears and his supposed killing. Christy takes an almost childish delight in the clothes. While he tries them on, Shawn becomes a pathetic/grotesque figure of fun with his own assumption that he too could be a hero by murder – the black comedy being extended here towards a further unlikelihood. Widow Quin's offering to marry Christy – to take him out of Shawn's way, reflects her own crafty nature (and certainly too her desperate need for a man). There is something predatory about the women in this play. While the Widow Quin propitiates him he indulges himself to the full, but by one of those sudden and ironic transitions Synge now has Mahon enter and tell his story, the true story. He is teased by Widow Quin (who has an eye to the main chance with Christy), and his revelations show the other side of Christy (is this reality or exaggeration?), the idle loafer who has been transformed by his own imagination and the acquired clothes into a playboy. The widow is also tormenting the hiding Christy, and Mahon's tale reduces him from hero to idle layabout to a failure with women, 'the loony'. The widow indulges her wit at the expense of Mahon, who damns Christy's appearance and is told that he is 'the spit of you'. She sends him off on a wild goose chase – a fine instance of dramatic irony here, since the audience knows what Mahon doesn't know, namely that Christy has heard it all. Christy is enraged because he has been found out and is no longer a hero but merely a liar. He also feels the loss of his position as potboy and with it the loss of Pegeen. His love for her is lyrically revealed and is treated with contempt by the widow. The latter's offer of help adds another possible layer of deception to the plot, but notice that she is also measuring usefulness to herself by Christy's working for her. At all times the simplicity and the economic bareness of the life is being emphasized. Expectation is of course aroused by the voices, Christy's promise to the widow being a sad poetic plaint which is soon reduced to practicalities by that earthy-minded woman. The move to get Christy to the sports is yet another display of the women's needs, but the act ends on a note of optimism from the widow – she may yet get her man.

cnuceen Little hill.
dray Low cart without sides for heavy loads.
supeen Little sip.
western world Here the province of Connaught on the Atlantic Coast. Compare eastern world in act three which is the province of Leinster.
lepping the stones Jumping across the stepping stones.
frish-frash Froth.
swaying and swiggling Pegeen's anger at Christy moves her to a graphic description of hanging that combines a poetic imagination with brutal realism, as so often in Synge.
Esau, Cain and Abel Esau had sold his birthright to Jacob for a 'mess of red pottage'; Cain murdered his brother Abel because his sacrifice was more acceptable to God. He thus became the first murderer. These are all Old Testament characters.
Neifin A mountain in Mayo.
Erris A district in the north-west of Mayo.
Circuit Judges Judges of the High Court who periodically visit assize towns to try the more serious cases.
mitch Skulk.
thraneen Piece of thread.
cleeve Basket.
Western States The United States of America. Note the constant play on western in western world, Western States. This symbolizes the vastness of the world beyond.
Kilmainham A jail in Dublin.
rye path Path by a rye field.
turbary Rights for cutting peat.
long car A type of wagon.
western world Here the United States. Compare the story in *The Aran Islands*, where the murderer is shipped to the United States. 'Western' is used in various senses during the play. Its reference is never precise but it can refer to Western Europe or merely the west coast of Ireland where the play is set.
It's the walking spirit This is a comic situation. But there is irony too, for the audience like Christy and the characters in the play have accepted the 'truth' of the murder.
streeler Idle oaf.
gob Mouth.
He takes off ... some pride It was this appearance of Old Mahon on the stage that upset the audience at the early

performances of the play. George Moore, the novelist, spoke of seeing 'disaster in that bloody bandage' when he read the play, and was proved right when the play was performed.

stuttering lout This reminds us of the change that has taken place in Christy.

lier on walls One who leans against walls whilst he talks to his friends.

felts Thrushes.

making mugs Making faces. Compare the beginning of the Act.

like an old weasel A graphic and appropriate image drawn from a close and accurate observation of nature.

seven and seventy divils In one of his notebooks used on a visit to Kerry, Synge refers to seven thousand and seventy devils. Synge borrowed extensively from his Kerry notebooks for *The Playboy*, even though the play is set in Mayo.

star of knowledge This idea is taken from Irish poetry, where it is frequently used. It may be a reference to love opening up new dimensions of experience, or a star that guides us.

spavindy ass A lame horse with diseased joints on its hind leg.

There's poetry talk Widow Quin pricks the bubble of Christy's poetic fervour. Both have their own conflicting sorts of reality.

hookers Cargo boats.

curagh Boat made of wicker-work covered with hide or canvas, widely used on the Atlantic coast.

wheel Spinning wheel.

boreen Lane.

making game Making fun.

Revision questions on Act 2

1 Compare Christy's version of the killing of his father in Act 1 with that given in Act 2.

2 Show how the relationship between Christy and Pegeen develops in Act 2.

3 Choose any two incidents in Act 2 and show how they are dramatically effective.

4 Describe the differences between Christy as described by his father and the Christy that we have seen during this Act.

Act 3

Old Mahon returns. Widow Quin cannot prevent the interest and suspicion he is arousing with his story of his attempted murder by his son. Christy's achievements as the champion Playboy of the Western World are graphically described by the watchers. When Christy wins the race, he is immediately recognized by Old Mahon. Widow Quin does her best to save the situation. Christy enters in triumph. Pegeen asserts the rights of her special relationship to him and seeks to protect him against the others' desire to congratulate him. Pegeen and Christy declare their love to each other. Michael, when he enters after furious drinking at the wake, gives his blessing to the marriage. Shawn is rejected; he cuts a contemptuous and cowardly figure.

At this point Old Mahon enters, and declares that he is Christy's father. Pegeen immediately turns on Christy. She is angry at the way he has deceived her. His achievements at the sports count for nothing. Mahon attacks Christy, but Christy chases him out with the loy. When he returns he is convinced that this time he has killed his father. So is the crowd, including Pegeen, who are determined to hang Christy for the murder. Widow Quin urges him to leave. He can think only of his love for Pegeen. Showing considerable strength and courage, he attacks the crowd, who seize him. Shawn then suggests scorching Christy's leg with burning peat, and while they are attempting this (as Christy bites, struggles and kicks), Old Mahon enters yet again. Christy and Old Mahon draw together against the rest. But the relationship is reversed. It is now Christy who is in charge. In a glorious burst of revelation, confidence and excitement, he finds himself and his true nature. Shawn approaches Pegeen and with grief she realizes that she has lost the only Playboy of the Western World.

Expectation is aroused by the description of the (unnamed) Christy's achievements at the sports. He has recovered his image, but the ominous passing of old Mahon by the window shows that the climax of confrontation (and hence the discrediting of Christy) is near. Before he appears the conversation between Jimmy and Philly dwells on the murder and its discovery, an ironic dimension which enhances the comedy of the fact that no murder was committed. There is the morbidity of the talk of skulls, which gives somehow the flavour (with the mention of 'an old Dane') of the gravedigger's scene in *Hamlet*. The whole of this death sequence has graphic symbolic overtones which suggest the fragile nature of existence.

Mahon's presence adds to the tension, and the widow Quin's role here is to try to ease the situation and placate him. But she also tells her own story of his madness in order to undermine whatever he may say with regard to Christy. Mahon's fluency is very like Christy's — like father like son — but he is a senior rogue in experience. Philly, perhaps inadvertently, almost provokes the situation before Christy enters. Widow Quin's description of Christy is of course at variance with Mahon's, and it virtually ensures that he will see his son. This brings about the climax of the play. Graphic description follows which successfully conveys the excitement of the race. The widow's actions and her insistence to Mahon that this is not his son makes him think that perhaps he is mad. This is another aspect of the black comedy. Again Mahon is apparently persuaded to leave.

Even at the moment of his triumph Christy still recurs to the murder he didn't commit, anxious to sustain his image in the eyes of these simple folk. Pegeen is possessive and 'radiant', a sure indication that she has completely taken over and been taken over by her image of Christy. The love exchanges are poetic and at times lyrical, interrupted by the noise of the drunken singing, the song about imprisonment carrying ominous overtones. The whole sequence is grotesque, as is Michael's account of the wake. The dispensation having (supposedly) arrived, this too is turned on its head by the passionate assertion by Pegeen that she is going to marry Christy. With Michael's agreement, we once again note the reversal of conventional practice – Pegeen is committed to a supposed murderer, while the respectable suitor is scorned. As he says, she has picked up 'a dirty tramp' and is rejecting even his reasonable material gifts.

With the departure of Shawn at the threat of physical violence Christy waxes eloquent and triumphant, unaware of the nemesis which will overtake him. Again Pegeen asserts her determination to marry Christy, Michael's response of joining their hands in mock ceremonial again partakes of the grotesque. It is followed by the dramatic entry of old Mahon and the beating of Christy. Pegeen, who has given her vows in effect, turns completely about in the ensuing hubbub, and Christy too turns on the crowd who are baiting him and putting him down. Notice the incidence of religious invocation at this stage. Christy has lost nothing in imaginative fluency, while Pegeen, humiliated, now goes for Mahon. Notice the superb crowd atmosphere at this stage. When Christy chases Mahon out of the door and then reappears we are not sure that he hasn't succeeded in committing the murder he had failed to commit earlier. Widow Quin once more tries to protect him against the crowd who think him guilty – a contrast with the notoriety Christy achieved earlier. Christy's obsession is only with Pegeen, but now there is a kind of hysteria, with Sara removing her petticoat for use in binding Christy. He now rages mad at the thought of separation from Pegeen, but the latter effects his capture, so complete is her own face-about. All is now dramatic action, struggling, violence on stage, with Pegeen as the ringleader and Shawn as assistant who gets his leg bitten for his pain. Nothing can stop Christy's mouth or his actions. Mahon sees capital in what has happened, for like Christy's story of his death, the story of the near hanging of Christy can be retailed by him up and down the land. Christy's triumph and his exit reduce Pegeen to what she was before – betrothed to Shawn and facing a passive life. Christy, for all his fantasy, has shown his real manhood at the end, triumphing over circumstances. The ending would appear to be largely optimistic.

trick-o'-the-loop man The man in charge of hoop-la.
cockshot-man The man that is 'shot' at in a sideshow.
A man can't hang The irony of this statement in brought out by Old Mahon's passing.
skelping Thrashing.
winkered Blinkered.
Belmullet A peninsula on the Mayo coast.
champion of the world The world is now narrowed down to what is happening in this small corner. This is symbolic of the way that Synge is making the events and feelings of this tiny village in rural Ireland representative of the world, transmuting the particular into the universal.
Watch him taking the gate This and similar speeches following play the part of a chorus in classical Greek tragedy where the action is described but not shown. It is in this way that Synge does not need any change of scene and preserves the classical unity of place.
There was one time Old Mahon had clearly suffered in the past from serious overdrinking. These are the sick fancies that came from delirium tremens.
lug Ear.
parlatic Paralytic.
union Workhouse, where the old and the destitute found shelter often in hard conditions.
blackthorn A walking stick made from the blackthorn shrub.
townland Area.
lonesome Again a reference to 'lonesome', with the image of even God feeling 'lonesome'. This is a constant theme with Christy and doubtless something of which Synge himself was always conscious.
when Good Friday's by When Lent is over. Making love and getting married were forbidden during Lent.
stretched back into your necklace George Roberts, in a broadcast in 1952, refers the origin of this phrase to an outing on Lough Bray when one of the party, Maire ni Garvey, leaned back into some flowers. This Synge described in words similar to those used in the play.

Lady Helen of Troy Helen, the wife of Menelaus, was taken by Hector to Troy. This was the cause of the Trojan Wars, as described by Homer, the greatest poet of Ancient Greece. Helen was a woman of incomparable beauty. One might well question whether a genuine peasant Christy could use the name of Helen of Troy so easily and appropriately.

Isn't there the light Christy suggests that it is Pegeen's beauty and his love for her that move him to 'such poet's talking, and such bravery of heart'.

in the darkness, spearing salmon i.e. poaching, an amusing juxtaposition of poetic fancy and reality.

paters Paternosters, our fathers, the Lord's Prayer.

with my gowns bought ready A sudden burst of practicality. The gown had been bought for her wedding to Shawn.

sailing the seas Again the imaginative widening of the horizon to the all-embracing image of 'the stars of God'.

turnkey Person in charge of prison keys.

Cavan town A market town in the County of Cavan.

retching speechless Michael's combination of revolting drunkenness with homage to the dead shows no sense of inappropriateness.

schemer i.e. depriving them out of the opportunity for a drunken wake similar to the one from which they have just returned.

gallous Fit for the gallows. These lines were given by one of the early performers as a specific example of a difficult part to express and words that required 'a great technique in feeling and expression'.

gaffer Still used in other dialects for boss, master, an idea emphasized by the extravagant image that follows.

fine words This indicates the high estimation in which these are held.

radiant lady Typical of the language of the folk ballad. Pegeen wants to raise the level of her speech, and attempts to do so by using such words as these.

plains of Meath Meath is an area of fertile farming country in the South-east.

Pharaoh's ma Pharaoh was an ancient Egyptian king. This is doubtless the recollection of a Bible story Pegeen may well have heard. The humour springs from her use of the word 'ma'.

mounted on the spring-tide Ironic, for Christy's luck is about to turn.

I'll not renege Ironic: she is about to turn against him.
What's a single man This passage is closely paralleled by one in *The Aran Islands*.
liar Christy plays on the two meanings of the word.
Munster A province including six counties, of which Kerry is one.
Crowd This speech expresses the central Greek idea of tragedy, the cutting down of the too proud man. Yet this is a comedy.
old hen Influenza
cholera morbus A disease causing vomiting and cramp.
pandied Beaten.
a drift of chosen females This is the famous line that lay at the root of the Playboy Riots with its implied slur on the virtue of Irish womanhood.
shifts Slips. This word caused an uproar and much subsequent discussion. Synge maintained it was a word in everyday use in the West of Ireland.
eastern world The province of Leinster in which Dublin is situated.
Lift a lighted sod Synge was urged to remove this part. The whole episode mirrors the ignorance and savagery of the Irish peasant.
picking cockles Unpleasant and badly paid work.

Revision questions on Act 3

1 Describe the final changes in Christy's character as shown in Act 3. Relate these changes to the events that cause or reveal them.
2 Outline the changes in the relationship of Christy and Pegeen in this Act. Make some reference to the quality of the language that mirrors the changing emotions.
3 Show how the relationship of Christy and Old Mahon develops in this Act.
4 Comment on the ending of the play and its effectiveness.
5 What part in the play is played by the sports?

The characters

Christy Mahon

'You've turned me a likely gaffer in the end of all, the way I'll go romancing through a romping lifetime from this hour to the dawning of the judgement day.'

The Playboy of the Western World is about the transformation of Christy Mahon from a shy, lonely, inarticulate young man into a courageous, confident, fluent hero. This is symbolized by his relationship with his father. Mahon, when he first speaks to Widow Quin about Christy describes him as 'a dirty, stuttering lout'. He is a layabout, a teller of foolish tales, content to lie in the sun, incompetent and lazy in his work. He is terrified of girls, and would run away from them and then spy on them from a hiding place. The girls would tease and mock him. He had a weak stomach, and the smell of strong drink was enough to make him drunk. A few puffs of strong tobacco would make him sick.

He has perhaps one virtue: he is a lover of little birds; and a love of nature is a sign of Synge's approval of a character: the audience are intended to sympathize with Christy. In appearance he is small, slender, dark and, when we first meet him, dirty. He is frightened and respectful in the way he addresses people.

Basking in the light of the interest shown in him by Michael, Pegeen and the drinkers, a new Christy begins to appear. From hesitant beginnings, a quality of surety and poetic imagination begins to emerge in his speech. He is quick to take offence when Pegeen says, 'A soft lad the like of you wouldn't slit the windpipe of a screeching sow.' Then the enormity of his professed deed comes out. He has killed his father. From this moment, the salvation of Christy begins: he acts up to the image expected of him, and, by the end of the play, the image has become the reality.

Of course he overplays the part. The murder is the key to the new life, and he refers to it to the point of weariness. Pegeen tells him sharply that she has heard 'that story six times since the dawn of day'. It is Christy's key to instant popularity. The local girls hang on his words and bring him gifts. It is the fact that he is 'wet and crusted with his father's blood' that makes Michael accept him as a son-in-law, for the murder is a guarantee of Christy's potency in breeding fine children.

But the murder is not the only factor. It is the cause and the opportunity but it is his love for Pegeen and hers for him that brings about the finer and surer change. Her admiration for him – whether it is for his small feet or 'quality' name or for his 'poet's talking' and his 'bravery of heart' – is always manifest. It is through love that he finds himself. During the course of the play his love changes. It is bound up with self-admiration in the early stages, the same sort of vanity that makes him look into a mirror and dwell on the comforts of his new position. This is a world away from the passionate, pleading intensity and urgency of his later love. Pegeen is the bridge that marks his movement from subservience to his father through dependence on Pegeen to his ultimate independence and self-sufficiency. He no longer needs the idea of 'two fine women fighting for the likes of me' to buttress his self-esteem.

The wheel has come full circle when he reverses the position between his father and himself. 'Go with you, is it? I will then, like a gallant captain with his heathen slave. Go on now and I'll see you from this day stewing my oatmeal and washing my spuds, for I'm master of all fights from now.' (Act 3) Like Old Mahon, the audience feels 'Glory be to God' when it sees this accomplished work of change, and sees Christy march into the glory of his new life.

Christy no longer needs the false prop of being his father's murderer. No longer need he be in the state when he is 'not able to say ten words without making a brag at the way he killed his father, and the great blow he hit with the loy.' For he has been in the sports 'the champion of the world'. He has had luck on his side abundantly and magnificently. 'There isn't a hap'orth isn't falling lucky to his hands today.' He has won not only all the prizes in the sports but 'the crowning prize' of Pegeen's hand in marriage. His talk has changed a peasant boy and girl into a king and queen, 'and any girl would walk her heart out before she'd meet a young man was your like for eloquence or talk at all,' Pegeen declares. (Act 3) They have indeed 'strained the bars of Paradise' to look on their love. Confidence, strength and passion flow from him. He has mastered his fate: 'I'm mounted on the spring-tide of the stars of luck, the way it'll be good for any to have me in the house.'

His new strength is to be tried. The crowd turn on him, and Pegeen rejects him, when Mahon shows that his status is founded on a lie. They fail to see that the lie has become the reality. 'There's the lad thought he'd rule the roost in Mayo.' Even Shawn comes into his own again. Now it is no challenge to single combat: he can – protected by the crowd's hostility to Christy – spitefully suggest the burning with the turf. It is Pegeen who blows the fire with a bellows and Pegeen who helps to drop the rope over his head. Yet Christy comes triumphantly through this trial. His courage never wavers. He finally conquers his last dependence – his love for Pegeen. Before the end of the play, the new Christy has been tried and proved.

Inevitably, critics have seen comparisons and symbols in Christy's transformation. The character does not need symbolic interpretation. It has sufficient depth, conviction and development in straightforward dramatic terms. The play has been compared to *Oedipus Rex*, by the ancient Greek writer of tragedies Sophocles – where the hero murders his father. There would seem little subsequent parallel between the fate of Oedipus and that of Christy, except that they both struggle through to ultimate nobility and salvation. But a blind, tragic, resigned Oedipus has little resemblance to the triumphant Christy of comedy eagerly embracing his future life. The Christ image has also been mentioned and, though the rejection of Christy may have elements in it of the betrayal and crucifixion of Christ, the similarity is an accidental one of situation. Philosophically, and in terms of experience and explanation, the two are poles apart.

The style should constantly remind us that Synge's achievement in the creation of the character of Christy is one of making a young peasant into a figure who represents all men in the expression of his feelings and the development of his real self.

Old Mahon

'My son and myself will be going our own way, and we'll have great times from this out telling stories of the villainy of Mayo, and the fools is here.'

It is difficult to get an accurate view of the character of Old Mahon until we can look back upon him and his part at the very end of the play. A great deal is said about him before he appears. The 'dead' Mahon is described as a farmer of substance who has little time for and no opinion of his lazy, good-for-nothing son. He was willing to sacrifice his son to get his hands on the house and money of the Widow Casey, even though she was old, ugly and shrewish. He brooks no opposition from his son to the marriage, even though the widow had wet-nursed Christy when he was born; and he threatens Christy roundly if he does not do as he is told.

Old Mahon is plainly a drunkard and, on his own description, his fancies in drink show him to have suffered from a state bordering on delirium tremens. When he finally appears, the reality corresponds to Christy's account of him. With his head in bandages, his threats of revenge, his alternation between rage and self-pity, he presents an unattractive picture. As Christy has nothing good to say about his father, so Old Mahon has only contempt for his son. He is no match for the

Widow Quin, who can throw his words back at him without his realizing what she is doing:

Widow Quin I'm thinking I seen him.
Mahon An ugly young blackguard.
Widow Quin A hideous fearful villain, and the spit of you. (Act 2)

It is plain that his contemptuous opinion and dictatorial ways have prevented his son's developing a life and character of his own. Because old Mahon is what he is, he has produced in Christy characteristics that lead to and justify his contempt. He is a bully, self-willed and selfish. His manner is such that it is almost possible for Widow Quin to convince the other men at the bar that he is out of his senses. And indeed such is his obsessional desire to revenge himself upon his son that he plays into her hands.

He feels himself, that he is 'the wrack and ruin of three-score years'. There is an element of the puppet in his appearances in the play. He is brought on and pushed off to fit the dramatic demands. His presences and absences heighten the tension and give excitement to the plot. He is the ghost of the past, of the old reality, always haunting Christy's new life. It is his appearance that destroys immediately and utterly the love between Pegeen and Christy. It is the 'killing' of Old Mahon that causes the crowd to turn against Christy: it is his final reappearance that leads to a resolution of the plot and Christy's triumph. He has a controlling part in the dénouement – not because of what he is but through his mere presence.

Finally, a little of the glory of Christy's salvation is reflected on him. He accepts the reversal of role between himself and his son. An elementary sense of loyalty makes him line up with Christy against the people of Mayo. Humbled, bereft of pride, anger and obsessions, perhaps he too has found, on a lower plane, a salvation that may make his final years better than his previous life.

Pegeen Mike (Margaret Flaherty)

'And I the fright of seven townlands for my biting tongue.'

Pegeen is a girl of about twenty, wild and beautiful in appearance. She is handsome enough to make credible Christy's ecstatic praise of her beauty. Christy, however, does not dwell on the details of her beauty. He is no Elizabethan sonneteer itemizing the charms of his mistress. She is the centre but not the substance of the rich imaginative sweep of his language. She is a young woman of pride and self-will. She is determined that she shall not be left in the shebeen on her own overnight. But it is on her own terms that she wishes to be protected, and she rejects Shawn and Widow Quin in favour of Christy, who, on any grounds of commonsense, as a stranger and a self-confessed murderer, could hardly be regarded as suitable company for a young girl on her own overnight.

She is no fragile heroine of romance, but a strong healthy young woman with her feet firmly on the ground. She may assert that her teeth are rattling with fear but Jimmy sees her as 'a fine, hardy girl would knock the head of any two men in the place'. Pegeen and Shawn Keogh will make an ill-matched pair. Her misfortune is that there is available no suitor of a spirit to match her own. Her contemptuous and low appraisal of him hardly seems a suitable basis on which to enter marriage. Doubtless she will develop a protectiveness towards him and his interests. Although she mocks and condemns him herself, she turns fiercely on Michael for doing so:

'What right have you to be making game of a poor fellow for minding the priest, when it's your own the fault is, not paying a penny pot-boy to stand along with me and give me courage in the doing of my work?'

It is Pegeen who attacks Christy on his very first appearance, calling him 'a soft lad' who has done nothing at all, and, in her mock rage, threatens to knock his head off. From the beginning she shows an interest in Christy that is plainly going to develop into love. She persuades him to stay, is concerned about his weariness after his long walk, admires his small feet, his name and his looks. She early reveals her jealousy and sees him 'walking the world telling out your story to young girls or old'. Her jealousy and anger are seen in all their glory when she discovers him drinking and linking arms with the girls and Widow Quin. Her scorn knows no bounds, and she attacks his gullibility, his new-found pride, and his repetition of the story of his father's murder. She cunningly plays on his fear by her description of hanging. However, when her anger has played itself out, she is determined that he shall not leave, and she realizes that a lad of spirit may give cause for jealousy.

The violence of Pegeen's temper can be seen in the quarrel with Widow Quin when she is determined that the Widow shall not stay the night. Her insults are personal, vindictive, and unrestrained. Perhaps Shawn is right when he says to Christy, 'She wouldn't suit you, and she with the devil's own temper the way you'd be strangling one another in a score of days.'

Yet she can also be diplomatic, and cunning, when the occasion demands. She knows the right time to approach her father to get his consent for her marriage to Christy, and her handling of her father on this occasion is a masterly example of forceful persuasion. Even in the most ecstatic moments of her love for Christy, she is still something of a realist. She asserts his coming is a miracle of God but she balances that thought by the observation that she has already bought her wedding dress. Her sense of reality makes her observe that 'we're only talking, maybe, for this would be a poor, thatched place to hold a fine lad is the like of you.'

It is a combination of pride and temper that destroys the love between Pegeen and Christy. Her cleverness and cunning are not sufficient to place in perspective his story about his father's murder, and to realize the man he has become. Her love is not independent of circumstance, and her pride and anger overwhelm it. 'It's there your treachery is spurring me on, till I'm hard set to think you're the one I'm after lacing in my heartstrings half an hour gone by.' Pegeen plays an active part in the group that lusts for Christy's blood. The sheer horror of her anger that has turned her love to hate comes out when she helps to drop the rope over his neck, and assists in the burning of his leg. There is indeed something unnatural and brutally savage in her character revealed at this stage. Her reaction can be interpreted not only in terms of pride and anger but also in a primitive lust for savage revenge. This Pegeen is a world away from the 'respectable and likeable country girl' that William Fay begged Synge to make of Pegeen.

There is a blending of comedy and tragedy when she boxes Shawn on the ear, then suddenly realizes her loss of Christy. Realization of their love comes too late, and her final cry has the quality of the tragic heroine. 'Oh, my grief, I've lost him surely. I've lost the only Playboy of the Western World.'

Widow Quin

'A widow woman, the like of me has buried her children and destroyed her man.'

Widow Quin is no witch, but in this small community she represents one. Evil stories about her are rampant; Pegeen accuses her of rearing a black ram at her own breast and doing away with her husband. She is cunning, but needs to be. She can hedge her bets by accepting bribes both from Shawn and Christy. She can desire Christy for herself yet make do with the promise of a right-of-way; a ram and a load of dung when she sees her pursuit of him is hopeless. During the early performances of *The Playboy* it was very obvious that the audience were very hostile to the characterization of Widow Quin.

She has a spirit of fun. She may be a widow and live in her

own cottage with its leaky thatch, but she can join in drinking with Christy and the girls with evident enjoyment. She has a very pretty wit too, and can mock Christy, old Mahon and Shawn without their realizing it. She is also a sympathetic listener: all the men find it very easy to speak to her about their problems. Although her own self-interest may make her a clever manipulator of men and situations, there is a warm-heartedness about her approach that gives a level of richness and humanity to her comic contribution that is quite different from Shawn's.

She looks upon the world and the people in it with a tolerant good humour. 'Well, if the worst comes in the end of all, it'll be a great game to see there's none to pity him but a widow woman, the like of me . . .' Her combination of tolerance and a sense of reality gives her a subtle understanding of men and women. Although she can appreciate, against her own interest, the imaginative flights of Christy's love for Pegeen, her sense of reality makes her comment, 'There's poetry talk for a girl you'd see itching and scratching, and she with a stale stink of poteen on her from selling in the shop.' She is not without imagination, though she can view her own situation, as well as that of other people, objectively and realistically.

Widow Quin, unlike Pegeen, has a shrewd understanding of Christy. When Old Mahon appears she is not surprised. It is significant that she places far more emphasis on Christy's actual achievement in the sports than does Pegeen. She it is who realizes that there is little resemblance between Christy, the son of Old Mahon, and the lad who is 'the wonder of the western world'. Her attempt to help Christy when all others have turned against him is a supreme instance of the irony of Synge's approach. There is outstanding virtue in her persistence in helping him when all the time he can speak only of his love for Pegeen.

On one level, Widow Quin has been presented as a schemer, a manipulator, a cynical observer of the baser feelings and actions; in the end she turns out to be charitable, warm-hearted and self-sacrificing. But she remains a character belonging to the world of farce rather than that of comedy, with her constant shifts from the glimmerings of warm humanity to the farcical search for bribes. Even in her best moments when she helps Christy to escape, Synge transforms the scene into farce by showing the widow's attempts to dress Christy in petticoats. She is an important device in the development of the plot, and performs some of the functions of the chorus in a Greek play – in her comments on the events and people in the play; in her objectivity; and in her realism and commonsense.

Shawn Keogh

Shawn Keogh is a poor thing. He has all the virtues – sobriety, faithfulness, religion; but they are all shown the wrong side out. He is a butt and a fool to other men – a figure of farce. He provides much of the humour of the play. The men despise him and mock his fears of spending the night at the shebeen for fear of Father Reilly. Shawn is an easy target for Christy's new-found manhood, for his cowardice is manifest to everyone. He is the occasion of humour in other men, but he is never a part of it: he is the target, not the instigator, of wit.

Shawn recognizes his own imperfections and is shameless in confessing them openly. When he speaks to Christy about Pegeen's temper, he – not without cunning as well as self-abasement – asserts, 'It's the like of me that she's fit for; a quiet simple fellow wouldn't raise a hand upon her if she scratched herself.'

Being base himself he assumes that everyone else is too. He thinks Christy may be bought off by bribes, and likes to think that he knows the price of every man and woman. But even in this he is mistaken, for he fails in the end to buy the support of the Widow Quin. There is little wonder that Pegeen should have few difficulties in persuading her father to let her wed

Christy in place of Shawn: the chances are indeed that he would father only 'puny weeds'. And, like all cowards, he has a streak of the bully in him. It is his peevish sense of cruelty that thinks up the refinements for the torturing of Christy. There is much laughter and little sympathy when Pegeen finally sends him on his way with a box on the ear. Our gratitude to him is only for the comedy that his presence in the play has provided.

Michael James Flaherty

'By the will of God, we'll have peace now for our drinks.'

He is the publican who likes his drink better than his daughter. He willingly leaves her alone overnight so that he can participate in the drinking which will be an important part of Kate Cassidy's wake. He prides himself on running a respectable house, yet sells illicit poteen. He is prepared to approve Pegeen's marriage to Shawn in spite of his contempt for him; but he turns quickly and easily to Christy when he sees Pegeen is set on him – it is the better match in terms of the essential qualities of the two men involved.

Flaherty has all the colour of language that he shares with the other characters in the play. He exemplifies the irony of the play's moral attitudes, where the murder of a father is regarded as a virtue. Yet he is not without his philosophy: he can moralize very prettily, if superficially; and he is full of little gobbets of wisdom about the single state, drinking, and the peaceful life.

'The will of God' figures largely in Flaherty's conversation, but little in his life. His ambition is to be regarded as a 'decent man', to drink in peace, and to be untroubled by the problems and evils of the world. He is likely to succeed, for he is highly adaptable and capable of making the best of any situation in which he finds himself.

Style

The writing of the play

Writing did not come easily to Synge. His plays are the result of much preparation, thought and hard work. The preparation went back to the notebooks he kept, recording the many expressions that pleased him in peasant speech. That is why he could maintain in his Preface that 'in writing *The Playboy of the Western World*, as in my other plays, I have used one or two words only that I have not heard among the country people of Ireland'. Yet the question of Synge's style is far more complex than this would suggest.

The writing of *The Playboy* was a laborious affair that took several years. Synge has told us something of his method of writing:

As to my manuscript, I work always with a typewriter – typing myself... I make a rough draft first and then work over it with a pen till it is nearly unreadable; then I make a clean draft again, adding whatever seems wanting, and so on... I really wrote parts of the last act more than eleven times, as I often tried out individual scenes and worked at them separately... Play writing is slow work.

Synge's allusions to the writing of the play speak constantly of the difficulties he was experiencing in completing it. Even at a late stage, he still thinks of revision:

It is more than likely that when I read it to you (Yeats) and Fay there will be little things to alter that have escaped me. And with my stuff it takes time to get even half a page of new dialogue fully into key with what goes before it.

The last act gave Synge special difficulty. 'I've been through Act 1,' he wrote. 'It is good I think and only needs a little more revision. I wish I could say the same for Act 3!' He talks about the play's not being finished, 'though in its last agony', and about its being 'provisionally finished'. During some periods of writing, Synge was very unwell, and the difficulties of getting the play right and finished contributed to his illness. 'I could not leave the Playboy,' he wrote, 'I am nearly in distraction with him and consequently am very unwell.' Making a plea for more time, he wrote to Lady Gregory, 'I would be very likely to knock up badly before I was done with him.'

Peasant speech

The largest influence upon Synge's style was peasant speech. He had read widely amongst continental writers and had been deeply influenced by the poetry of Wordsworth, but the one constant and abiding factor in his writing was his use of dialect. Yeats asserted that he was hardly aware of the existence of other writers.

A battle has always raged over the degree to which Synge reproduced peasant speech in his plays. James Joyce asserted that he wrote 'a kind of fabricated language as unreal as his characters were unreal', and he tells the story of a friend who went to stay in the west of Ireland and was bitterly disappointed when he returned. 'I did not hear one phrase of Synge all the time I was down there. Those characters only exist on the Abbey stage. And St John Ervine called him a 'faker of peasant speech'.

Oliver St John Gogarty asserted,

This language I have never heard in the mouth of any countryman in Ireland. It is an ersatz, which has been credited with much simplicity and beauty, but which has always offended me by its artificiality.

The answer is that Synge took from Irish peasant speech exactly what he wanted. It is the inspiration behind his style, but it is not the whole of it. It is what Synge made of his use of dialect that is crucial. He delighted in hearing, recording and using any good phrase that he heard.

Yeats was to write:

John Synge, I and Augusta Gregory thought
All that we did, all that we said or sang
Must come from contact with the soil

The dialect was a source, a stimulus to his style. Without this inspiration, it is doubtful whether Synge would have written anything that would not now be forgotten. It is the fusion of the peasant speech and his own art and personality that constitutes the greatness of Synge.

He was writing plays in peasant speech and about peasant life for a relatively sophisticated Dublin audience. Very few of his audience would know the differences of dialect in the various parts of Ireland. Indeed Synge himself did not make any distinction. Although *The Playboy* is set in Mayo, Synge had spent very little time there and his knowledge of dialect was based on stays in Aran, Wicklow and other parts of Ireland.

Vocabulary and use of words

It is also a mistake to regard Synge's style as a whole, and an evolutionary development. In *Riders to the Sea* the economical style is very different from the rich joyous imaginative approach of *The Playboy*, which is different again from the rhythmic experiment undertaken in *Deirdre of the Sorrows*. Synge's style is matched to the purpose and mood of the individual play – an indication of his sensitive awareness and of his mastery of his language and technique.

'In a good play,' Synge asserts in the Preface, 'every speech should be as fully flavoured as a nut or an apple and such speeches cannot be written by anyone who works among people who have shut their lips on poetry.' Synge's own attitude is ambivalent, and it is dangerous to attempt to select in the plays words or phrases that he must have added to peasant speech. When he was approached by a representative of the press who questioned whether words such as 'potentate' and 'retribution' were typical of speech in places where the play was set, Synge replied laughing that that was 'just the very place to hear them'. He knew peasants such as he had tried to depict, taking the keenest delight in airing any big words of which they had got hold. As an instance, he said, he heard a poor old woman who was absolutely illiterate say, 'I have used all sorts of stratagems to keep the hens out.'

Synge had a special interest in the texture and life of the individual word. Padraic Colum, the Irish poet, spoke to him about 'the gorgeousness of the dialogue' in Synge's plays. 'Ah', replied Synge, 'but if you were to see it when it comes out first, it's just bald!'

That words become worn out was one of Synge's theories. He hated to see writers like Ibsen and Zola 'dealing with the reality of life in joyless and pallid words'. Far from being a purist in this selection of dialect, Synge was not too worried about the sources of his words. He was as likely to ransack seventeenth-century English as Irish peasant dialect. Indeed, so immersed did he become in the language of seventeenth-century England that it led to his finding considerable difficulty in the correct spelling of modern English.

In prose drama the words are only the medium for the sense; in poetic drama the words have their own majesty and give their own delight. The language of Synge, although prose, has the qualities of poetry. He loves the devices of poetry, such as alliteration. 'Drink a health to the *w*onders of the *w*estern *w*orld, the *p*irates, *p*reachers, *p*oteen-makers, with the *j*obbing *j*ockies, *p*arching *p*eelers . . .'

His language can take flight whether under the inspiration of insult or of love:

Doesn't the world know you treated a black ram at your own breast . . . Doesn't the world know you've been seen shaving the foxy skipper from France for a three-penny bit and a sop of grass tobacco would wring the liver from a mountain goat you'd meet leaping the hills?'

'It's little you'll think if my love's a poacher's, or an earl's itself, when you'll feel my two hands stretched around you, and I squeezing kisses on your puckered lips, till I'd feel a kind of pity for the Lord God is all ages sitting lonesome in His golden chair.'

He can rise to the ecstasy of: 'And making mighty kisses with our wetted mouths, or gaming in a gap of sunshine, with yourself stretched back unto your necklace, in the flowers of the earth.'

Rhythm is one of the qualities of poetry, as well as its imaginative play, delight in words, and poetic vitality. The rhythm is pronounced but it is constant in all characters. The actors in the first production found the rhythm difficult to master.

Use of dialect

1. Use of the present participle:
   'It should be larceny, *I'm thinking*.'
   'Where will you find the likes of them, *I'm saying*?'
2. 'the like of' for 'like':
   'A soft lad *the like of* you wouldn't slit the wind-pipe of a screeching sow.'
   'With a kind of quality name, *the like of* what you'd find on the great powers...'
3. Omission of 'who, that, which' (relative pronouns):
   'A lad would kill his father, I'm thinking, would face...'
4. unusual use of 'and':
   'Wasn't I telling you, *and* you a fine handsome fellow...'
5. use of 'it's':
   '*It's* a wonder, Shaneen, the Holy Father'd be taking notice of the likes of you.'
6. use of imperative (command):
   'And *let* you go off till you'd find a radiant lady.'

7 use of the word 'after':
  'He's *after* dying on me.'
8 Use of reflexive pronoun (—self):
  '*Himself* will stop along with you.'
  '*Herself* will be safe this night.'
  '*Itself*' often means 'actually'.
9 Reported questions as direct questions:
  'Wait till you see is he the lad I think.'
10 Characteristic words:
  '*decent*', '*swearing Christians*', '*destroying*', '*world*'.
11 Unusual words and expressions:
  '*drunken* all the wealth and wisdom', '*noon of Mary*'.

Synge consistently and deliberately avoids the use of conventional stage Irish, recognized colloquialisms from Anglo-Irish, or city (Dublin) slang. Thus we never find 'me' for 'my', 'yous' for 'you', or the word 'sure'.

General questions and sample answer in note form

1 Describe Synge's use of dialect in this play.
2 Choose any *two* incidents in the play that you consider good examples of effective dramatic situations. Describe them and state what contribution they make to the play as a whole.
3 Trace the development of Christy's character.
4 What elements in the play do you regard as out of place in a comedy?
5 What picture of peasant life is given in the play?
6 Christy's love for Pegeen is the one noble thing in *The Playboy of the Western World*. Comment on this statement.
7 A strange juxtaposition of brutality and beauty is one of the marks of the play. Discuss.
8 How far is the character of Pegeen convincing?
9 Shawn Keogh is the source of all the comedy in the play. Discuss.
10 Widow Quin shows that Synge's characterization transcends any conventional bounds between good and bad. Discuss.
11 In what ways does Christy resemble (a) Widow Quin and (b) Old Mahon?
12 Show how Synge uses the unities of time, action and place to add to the effectiveness of the play.
13 'You've turned me a likely gaffer in the end of all.' What special contributions have various characters made to Christy's development?
14 What features in the play might have offended the audiences who attacked *The Playboy* during its first production?
15 A strange combination of reality and fantasy. Comment on this estimate of the play.

Suggested notes for essay answer to question 1

Introduction – indicate clearly that Synge is combining authenticity and poetry in his particular usages – choose some single-word/phrase examples to give the range.

(i) Take half a dozen examples from the language of Christy and show exactly what effects are achieved – his individual usages – vividness – poetry – relaxed/natural speech (or supposedly natural speech) – earthiness – violence, etc.

(ii) Apply the same test to Pegeen and Widow Quin – dialect indicative of occupation – of the fact that they are women – innuendo – economic – sexual, etc.

(iii) Now consider the usages of old Mahon and Michael or Shawn – what does dialect tell you of character? – social position? – motivation – what does it contribute to atmosphere, etc.?

Conclusion – choose examples of dialect which illustrate that without them the play would be the poorer – authenticity diminished – illusion not sustained, etc.

Demonstrate that the dialect acts as a shared experience of life and communication between the characters.

Further reading

The Aran Islands, amongst Synge's prose work, will provide a background to the play and its atmosphere. Of the other plays the short *Riders to the Sea* is certainly the best and most illuminating. *The Shadow of the Glen* is a comedy that provides a comparison to *The Playboy of The Western World* as is *The Tinker's Wedding*. Synge wrote only seven plays altogether. These are published in the Everyman's Library (Dent), which includes the plays, the poems and a selection from *The Aran Islands*. Four of the plays and *The Aran Islands* are published in the World's Classics (Oxford). The Complete Works are published in four volumes by Oxford University Press. The fourth volume, which contains *The Playboy of the Western World*, is edited by A. Saddlemyer, and contains an introduction that gives valuable insight into Synge's method of working and the background to the play.
The Plays and Poems of J. M. Synge, edited by T. R. Henn (Methuen University Paperback) is an excellent annotated edition of the works.

Books about Synge

J. M. Synge and Lady Gregory, Elizabeth Coxhead (Longman's Writers and Their Work: No. 149) A useful short introduction.
J. M. Synge and His World, Robin Skelton (Thames & Hudson) This book contains all the necessary information about Synge's life, and has a large number of illustrations that add considerably to the reader's understanding of his background
Interviews and Recollections, ed. E. H. Mikhail (Macmillan) This selection of writings about Synge by those who knew him gives the reader an invaluable insight into the writer as well as the Irish theatre.

For background on the Irish dramatic movement at the Abbey Theatre

The Irish Dramatic Movement, Una M. Ellis-Fermor (Methuen).

Brodie's Notes

TITLES IN THE SERIES

Jane Austen	**Pride and Prejudice**
Robert Bolt	**A Man for All Seasons**
Emily Brontë	**Wuthering Heights**
Charlotte Brontë	**Jane Eyre**
Geoffrey Chaucer	**Prologue to the Canterbury Tales**
Geoffrey Chaucer	**The Nun's Priest's Tale**
Geoffrey Chaucer	**The Wife of Bath's Tale**
Geoffrey Chaucer	**The Pardoner's Prologue and Tale**
Charles Dickens	**Great Expectations**
Gerald Durrell	**My Family and Other Animals**
T. S. Eliot	**Selected Poems**
George Eliot	**Silas Marner**
F. Scott Fitzgerald	**The Great Gatsby** and **Tender is the Night**
E. M. Forster	**A Passage to India**
John Fowles	**The French Lieutenant's Woman**
Anne Frank	**The Diary of Anne Frank**
William Golding	**Lord of the Flies**
Graham Handley (ed)	**The Metaphysical Poets: John Donne to Henry Vaughan**
Thomas Hardy	**Far From the Madding Crowd**
Thomas Hardy	**Tess of the D'Urbervilles**
Thomas Hardy	**The Mayor of Casterbridge**
Aldous Huxley	**Brave New World**
John Keats	**Selected Poems and Letters of John Keats**
Philip Larkin	**Selected Poems of Philip Larkin**
D. H. Lawrence	**Sons and Lovers**
Laurie Lee	**Cider with Rosie**
Harper Lee	**To Kill a Mockingbird**
Arthur Miller	**The Crucible**
Athur Miller	**Death of a Salesman**
George Orwell	**1984**
George Orwell	**Animal Farm**
J. B. Priestley	**An Inspector Calls**
J. D. Salinger	**The Catcher in the Rye**
William Shakespeare	**The Merchant of Venice**
William Shakespeare	**King Lear**
William Shakespeare	**A Midsummer Night's Dream**
William Shakespeare	**Twelfth Night**
William Shakespeare	**Hamlet**
William Shakespeare	**As You Like It**
William Shakespeare	**Romeo and Juliet**
William Shakespeare	**Julius Caesar**
William Shakespeare	**Macbeth**
William Shakespeare	**Antony and Cleopatra**
William Shakespeare	**Othello**
William Shakespeare	**The Tempest**

George Bernard Shaw	**Pygmalion**
Alan Sillitoe	**Selected Fiction**
John Steinbeck	**Of Mice and Men** and **The Pearl**
Alice Walker	**The Color Purple**

ENGLISH COURSEWORK BOOKS

Terri Apter	**Women and Society**
Kevin Dowling	**Drama and Poetry**
Philip Gooden	**Conflict**
Philip Gooden	**Science Fiction**
Margaret K. Gray	**Modern Drama**
Graham Handley	**Modern Poetry**
Graham Handley	**Prose**
Graham Handley	**Childhood and Adolescence**
R. J. Sims	**The Short Story**